Book bri

1. *The Canterbury Tales* is a collection of stories written in English by Geoffrey Chaucer between 1387 and 1400.

2. People say it's Chaucer's greatest work and one of the most important works in English literature.

3. The book is about a group of pilgrims. Each of them tells a story as they travel from London to Canterbury to visit the shrine of Saint Thomas à Becket at Canterbury Cathedral.

4. Through the stories, Chaucer gives us an ironic and critical picture of English society at that time and in particular of the Church.

5. Chaucer uses different kinds of people to tell the stories to show us what 14th century England was like.

www.eligradedreaders.com

In this reader:

21st Century Skills	To encourage students to connect the story to the world they live in.
Movers	A1 level activities.
Story Notes	A brief summary of the text.
Glossary	Explanation of difficult words.
Picture Caption	A brief explanation of the picture.
Audio	These icons indicate the parts of the story that are recorded. start / stop
Think	To encourage students to develop their critical thinking skills.

The FSC® certification guarantees that the paper used in these publications comes from certified forests, promoting responsible forestry management worldwide.

FSC www.fsc.org MIX Paper from responsible sources FSC® C127663

For this series of ELI graded readers, we have planted 5000 new trees.

Geoffrey Chaucer

The Canterbury Tales

Retold and Activities by
Michael Lacey Freeman

Illustrated by
Simone Massoni

Teen ELi Readers

Teen Eli Readers

The **ELI Readers** collection is a complete range of books and plays for readers of all ages, ranging from captivating contemporary stories to timeless classics. There are four series, each catering for a different age group: **First ELI Readers, Young ELI Readers, Teen ELI Readers** and **Young Adult ELI Readers**. The books are carefully edited and beautifully illustrated to capture the essence of the stories and plots. The readers are supplemented with 'Focus on' texts packed with background cultural information about the writers and their lives and times.

The Canterbury Tales
By Geoffrey Chaucer
Retold and Activities by
Michael Lacey Freeman
Language Level Consultant
Janet Borsbey, Ruth Swan and Silvana Sardi
Illustrated by **Simone Massoni**

ELI Readers
Founder and Series Editors
Paola Accattoli, Grazia Ancillani, Daniele Garbuglia (Art Director)

Graphic Design
Andersen the Premedia Company

Production Manager
Francesco Capitano

Photo credits
Gettyimages, Shutterstock

New edition: **2021**
First edition: **2014**

P.O. Box 6
62019 Recanati (MC)
Italy
T +39 071750701
F +39 071977851
info@elionline.com
www.elionline.com

Typeset in 12 / 17 pt
Fulmar designed by Leo Philp

Printed in Italy by
Tecnostampa - Pigini Group Printing Division
Loreto - Trevi
ERT 114.10
ISBN 978-88-536-3185-5

Contents

THE Canterbury TALES CHARACTERS

The Knight
Everybody likes him and he's always happy to help people.

The Clerk
A nice man who doesn't speak much. He loves reading and studying.

The Merchant

He has a lot of money but he isn't happy.

The Franklin

A very rich, important man with a big house in the country.

The Pardoner

He says prayers for people if they give him money.

Before you read

Grammar

1 Read a part of a letter. Complete the letter with the verbs below.

~~am~~	are	is	know	tells	travel	want

I'*m* reading *The Canterbury Tales*, by Geoffrey Chaucer. Do you (**1**) ___ anything about this book? Chaucer wrote this book in 1387. At this time, God was very important for many people. People often went on pilgrimages. You go on a pilgrimage when you (**2**) ___ to an important town or city. People go on a pilgrimage because they (**3**) ___ to be near to God. In Chaucer's book, a group of people go on a pilgrimage to Canterbury. Canterbury (**4**) ___ a town in England. Everybody in this group (**5**) ___ a story. These stories (**6**) ___ the Canterbury Tales.

2 Complete the sentences with the verbs below.

buy	~~look~~	study	talk	work	pay

The Knight: *Look* at the men in the picture on page 27. That's my job. Don't worry! The group is safe with me.

1 **The Clerk:** I'm a student and I _______ all the time.
2 **The Merchant:** I have a business. I _______ things, and then people _______ for the things I buy.
3 **The Franklin:** I have a big farm. A lot of people _______ on my farm.
4 **The Pardoner:** I _______ to people about God. I help them to be near to God.

Reading and Writing MOVERS

3 Choose the correct word for each sentence about people from the stories.

Emily ___*is*___ a beautiful, young girl in the Knight's Tale.

are am ~~is~~

1 Walter is in the Clerk's Tale. Everybody ________ what he says.

do does don't

2 Damien is in the Merchant's Tale. He ________ for a man with a lot of money.

work does works

3 Does Damien ________ a good job?

have has is

4 Dorigen is in the Franklin's Tale and she ________ near the sea

has lives leaves

5 Ames is in the Pardoner's Tale and he ________ having fun.

goes wants likes

Speaking

21st Century Skills

4 This book is called *The Canterbury Tales*. Look on the Internet and answer these questions.

1 Which part of England is Canterbury in?

____

2 What does 'Tale' mean?

____

3 Who was Thomas à Becket and what happened to him?

____

4 Why is Canterbury Cathedral important?

____

5 Who was Geoffrey Chaucer?

____

Chapter 1

The Prologue

2 It's a beautiful day! The weather is good. The birds are singing. The grass is green, and there are flowers everywhere. Now, my story can begin. My name's Geoffrey. Today, I'm going on a pilgrimage[1] to Canterbury. I'm going to Canterbury with a group of people. We're going there together. I met these people yesterday, at an inn[2], in London.

Geoffrey Chaucer stops at an inn in London before starting his pilgrimage to Canterbury.

I arrived[3] at the inn in the afternoon. I was very tired, and hungry. 'Good afternoon!' I said to the man who worked at the inn. He was the innkeeper. 'I'd like a room for the night. I'm going to Canterbury tomorrow. The road to Canterbury is long. I need to sleep well before I start.'

'Good afternoon,' said the innkeeper. 'Do you know that some other people are going to Canterbury tomorrow? They're staying here tonight.'

'I'd like to meet them,' I said to the innkeeper.

[1] **pilgrimage** when you go to a special place to be near to God
[2] **inn** a place to sleep, and to eat and drink
[3] **to arrive** to travel and then find the place that you want to go to

In the evening, I met the other people. The inn was big and there was a lot of good food and drink. Everybody had dinner together. The innkeeper gave good food to everybody. The innkeeper was a nice person. He was a very big man and he enjoyed speaking to people. He was very good at his job. Everybody enjoyed their dinner.

After dinner, the innkeeper spoke to the group. 'You're a very nice group of people,' he said. 'I know that God wants to listen to your prayers[1]. You're all going to the same place, so, you must go to Canterbury together. What do you think?'

'Yes, we can go together!' I said.

'I want to go to Canterbury with you,' said the innkeeper. 'Now, we have to travel for a long time. I think we can do something interesting[2]. We can play a game. What do you think?'

'Yes!' said everybody in the group. 'Tell us about this game.'

'Now, listen to what I have to say,' said the innkeeper. 'We can go to Canterbury together.

Geoffrey has dinner with the other people who want to go to Canterbury and the innkeeper says he wants to go with them. He says that they can play a game on their way to Canterbury.

[1] **prayer** when you talk to God, you say a prayer
[2] **interesting** something you enjoy

Everybody must tell a story and the innkeeper wants to give the person with the best story a free dinner at his inn. Everybody likes the idea.

Every person can tell a story[1]. I want to listen to every story. Then I can tell you which story is the best.' Everybody in the group wanted to play this game. 'Very well,' said the innkeeper. 'I want to give something to the person who tells the best story. That person can have dinner at my inn. I want to pay for the dinner.'

The people in the group were very happy. They began to think of what story to tell. In the group there was a Knight. Everybody liked him. He was always happy to help people. He was an important man, but his clothes were cheap. His horse was fast, but it was small.

The Knight says his story is about two brothers who love the same woman.

'I'm a Knight, and my life is very exciting,' said the Knight. 'My story is also exciting. It's about two brothers who love the same woman.'

There was also a Clerk in the group. He was a nice man, but he didn't speak very much. He liked reading and studying. That's all he wanted to do. He was very slim and he didn't eat very much. He liked books more than food.

[1] **story** when you tell someone about something that happened in the past

›

The Pardone[r] is saying a prayer.

The Clerk likes reading and his story is about a King with many secrets.

'I read a lot of books,' said the Clerk. 'I don't want nice clothes or good food. I don't have much money. I use the money I have to buy books. That's why I read a lot of stories. My story is very easy to understand, but, it's not boring. It's about a King[1] who has many secrets[2].'

Another[3] person in the group was a Merchant. He had a lot of money. But he wasn't a happy man. He always had a sad face. He was different from the Knight. His clothes were very expensive. Everything he had was expensive: his clothes, his hat, and his horse.

The Merchant has a lot of money but he's sad. His story is also sad about an old man who can't see.

'I have an important business,' said the Merchant. 'And I have a lot of things to do. But I'm not very happy with my life. That's why my story is sad. It's about an old man who can't see.'

I also have to tell you about another man. He was a Franklin. He was different from the Clerk. He was very rich[4] and important, but he didn't have a business. He had a big house in the country.

[1] **King** 
[2] **secret** something that you don't want other people to know
[3] **another** one more
[4] **rich** a person who has a lot of money

He often invited people there. He liked good food.

'I'm very old. My house is big. I like inviting people there,' said the Franklin. 'In my house, I often tell stories. I enjoy it. My story is very interesting. It's about a woman who doesn't like the sea. Why doesn't she like the sea? Well, you have to listen to my story.'

The Franklin is very rich and invites people to his big house. His story is about a woman who doesn't like the sea.

There's another person I want to tell you about. He was a Pardoner. He also liked reading. He liked to sing songs and say prayers. He had a strange[1] face.

'I travel a lot and I always say prayers for people,' said the Pardoner. 'There are a lot of bad people in the world. I say prayers for them, but they have to give me some money. My story is about three people who do something very bad.'

The Pardoner says prayers for people who give him money. His story is about three people who do something bad.

Everybody was very tired. It was late in the evening, and the Knight said, 'We can go to bed now. Then we can leave early in the morning.' We all went to bed. We were tired, but happy.

Early next morning, we got up. Then we

[1] **strange** (here) unusual for this person

The next morning, they leave for Canterbury. They stop to have something to eat and the Knight says he wants to be the first to tell his story.

left for Canterbury on our horses. We were slow. After many hours we came to a place called Saint Thomas and we stopped there.

We sat down, then we had something to eat. After eating, the innkeeper said, 'Listen, do you remember what we said last night?'

'Of course,' said the Knight.

'Well,' said the innkeeper, 'who wants to begin? Who wants to tell the first story?'

'I'm happy to tell you my story,' said the Knight. 'It's very exciting.'

The Knight began to tell his story.

Think

Which story do you think sounds the most interesting?

The innkeep… asks who wants to be the first to te… their story.

Reading Comprehension

1 Match the descriptions of each story.

1 [b] The Pardoner's story is about three men
2 ☐ The Franklin's story is about a woman
3 ☐ The Knight's story is about two brothers
4 ☐ The Merchant's story is about an old man
5 ☐ The Clerk's story is about a King

a who doesn't like the sea.
~~**b**~~ who do something very bad.
c who love the same woman.
d who has many secrets.
e who can't see.

Writing

2 Complete the sentences using some of the adjectives from Chapter 1

bad	big	expensive	fast	~~hungry~~	old	slim

Geoffrey was very tired and *hungry* .
1 The Knight's horse was ________ .
2 The Clerk didn't eat very much, and he was very ________ .
3 The Merchant's horse was very ________ .
4 The Franklin was an ________ man.
5 The Franklin had a ________ house.
6 The Pardoner said that there are a lot of ________ people in the world.

Speaking and Writing

21st Century Skills

3 The people in the book must all tell a story. Talk to a partner and answer these questions.

1 What kind of books do you like reading in your free time?
2 How important do you think it is to read? Why?
3 Where do you like reading?
4 Do you like ebooks more than paper ones? Why? /Why not?
4 How often do you read comics like the ones in this picture?

Before-reading Activities

Reading and Writing

MOVERS

4 Look at this picture from Chapter 2. Complete the sentences and answer the questions.

The woman is in the garden.
1 The woman has got blond ______.
2 Who's watching her? ______
3 How many flowers are there in the woman's right hand? ______
4 What's the woman doing? ______

Listening

3 **5 Listen to the first part of Chapter 2. Cross out the incorrect option.**

The *Knight* / ~~*the Merchant*~~ told the first story.
1 The two brothers were *clerks* / *knights*.
2 They were from *Thebes* / *Athens*.
3 They were *happy* / *sad*.
4 They lived in *Thebes* / *Athens*.

Chapter 2

The Knight's Tale

3 "My story is about two brothers," said the Knight. "Their names were Palamon and Arcite, and they were knights. The brothers were from a city called Thebes. They did everything together. They weren't only brothers; they were also friends, but they were very sad."

"They were sad because they didn't live in Thebes any more. They lived in Athens. They didn't live in a house; they lived in a prison[1]. They couldn't leave the prison and they couldn't speak to anybody. Every morning, they looked out of the prison window. From their window, they could see a beautiful garden."

The knight starts telling his story about two brothers in prison in Athens.

4 One morning, Palamon woke up and then he looked out of the window, but something was different. There was a woman in the garden. Her name was Emily. She was the daughter of the King of Athens.

[1] **prison** look at the picture on page 23. Palamon lives here, in a prison

'Look!' said Palamon. 'That woman is beautiful. Oh! I'm in love! Arcite! Come here! Look!'

Arcite went to the window and he saw the woman. 'Yes, you're right. She is beautiful,' he said. 'One day, I want to marry[1] her.'

Arcite and Palamon see the King's daughter, Emily, in the garden and they both want to marry her one day.

'I saw her first!' said Palamon. 'You can't love her. You must help me!'

'No!' said Arcite. 'My love is perfect[2]. You must help me!'

Arcite and Palamon both loved Emily. They had the same conversation every day. 'I love her!' No! You can't love her!' was all you could hear; from the small room, their prison.

Then one day, a friend of Arcite's visited the King of Athens. He wanted to speak to the King about Arcite. 'Can he go home?' asked Arcite's friend. 'He's a good man. I want to see him again.'

'Alright,' said the King. 'Arcite can go home, but he must never come to Athens again. Palamon must stay in prison.'

Arcite went back to Thebes, but he wasn't happy. 'I'm going home,' thought Arcite. 'But,

[1] **to marry** when you want a husband or wife you do this
[2] **perfect** when nothing is wrong

I can't see Emily. Palamon can see her in the garden. It's better in prison.'

The King lets Arcite go home but he mustn't come back to Athens. Arcite is sad because he can't see Emily anymore. Palamon is in prison and can see her in the garden.

But Palamon was sad as well. 'Arcite, you can come back to Athens,' he thought. 'You can fight[1] the King of Athens, and you can marry Emily. I have to stay in this prison.'

In Thebes, Arcite was very sad; he didn't sleep or eat very much. 'I must wait for two years,' thought Arcite. 'Then I can go to Athens again. Nobody will know me then. I can wear different clothes. I can change my name. I can find a job. I can be a servant[2] in the King's house. Then I can see Emily.'

After two years Arcite goes back to Athens. He meets his brother Palamon in the forest. Palamon still loves Emily too.

That's why, after two years, Arcite went back to Athens. He was the King's servant. The King liked Arcite because he was good at his job. One day, Arcite went to the forest[3] near Athens. And he sat near a tree. 'What can I do?' said Arcite. 'I'm the King's servant. I'm near Emily, but she doesn't know who I am. I want to die!'

Then a man spoke to Arcite. It was Palamon! 'Hello, brother! It's me!' said Palamon. 'Stop thinking about Emily! Only I can love her.'

›

The knight looks at Emi from his prison. He thinks she's very beautif and wants tc marry her.

[1] **to fight** look at the picture on page 27. The people are fighting
[2] **servant** somebody who works for the King
[3] **forest** a place where there are a lot of trees

'Palamon, it's you!' said Arcite. 'Why aren't you in prison?'

'The King sent me home yesterday, but I'm not going home. I want to find Emily.'

'Well, I must fight you for Emily,' said Arcite. 'But not today. We're knights remember? We must do things in the right way. Tonight, I want to bring[1] some food, then tomorrow we can fight.'

'Alright,' said Palamon. So the brothers said goodbye. The next day, they met in the forest. And then they started fighting.

The brothers say goodbye and meet in the forest the next day. The King is also in the forest. He's with Emily and sees Palamon and Arcite.

On the same day, the King was also in the forest. He was with Emily. He saw Palamon and Arcite. 'Stop!' said the King. 'What are you doing? Stop now!'

'Kill[2] us!' said Arcite. 'Now, I'm your servant. Before that I was in your prison. My name's Arcite and this is my brother Palamon. We're fighting because we both love Emily.'

'Then you must die!' said the King.

But Emily stopped the King. 'Please don't kill them!' she said. 'They're fighting for love.'

[1] **to bring** to take something with you
[2] **to kill** to do something so that somebody dies

'Well,' said the King. 'You're right, Emily. But only one of them can marry you. Palamon, Arcite, come back to the forest next summer. Bring a hundred knights. Then you can fight for Emily. Now, go!'

Soon it was summer. Palamon and Arcite came back to Athens. They both had a hundred knights. They were ready to fight the next day.

The two brothers start to fight but the King sees them in the forest. At first he wants to kill them but Emily says they're fighting for love, so the King tells them to come back next summer with 100 knights each to fight for Emily.

That night, Palamon had a dream[1]. In his dream a woman said, *'I can see you. You're marrying Emily.'*

On the same night, Arcite also had a dream. In his dream a man said, *'I can hear you. You're saying, Hooray! Emily can be my wife.'*

Which dream was right? Well, now I want to tell you.

In the morning, everybody came to the forest. The knights were ready and they began to fight!

After three hours, Emily was worried. 'They're fighting for me! Who will be my husband? How long must they fight?'

After many hours, they stopped. Palamon was very tired. 'Stop!' he said. 'I can't fight any more!'

[1] **dream** what you think about when you sleep

Both brothers dream that Emily can be their wife, but in the end Arcite dies and Palamon marries Emily.

'Stop fighting!' said the King. 'Arcite will be Emily's husband.'

'Hooray!' said Arcite. 'I'm very happy. Emily can be my wife. I must go to her and ... but then, Arcite stopped speaking. He didn't feel well.

People came to help Arcite. 'I'm not well,' said Arcite. 'I can't ... I can't feel anything. I'm dying. This is the end. Goodbye Emily, my love. Goodbye Palamon, my brother.'

And then, Arcite died.

• • •

Soon, it was winter. The King called for Palamon and Emily.

'As you know, Arcite died last summer, and it was very sad,' said the King. 'Emily, I want you to be happy. Palamon, you must marry Emily. It's the right thing to do.'

'Thank you!' said Palamon. 'Arcite was a good knight. He was my dear brother, but, we had to fight for love. Emily, I know we must be happy together, but we must never forget my brother. He died for love.'

Think

What did you like and not like about the knight's story?

Arcite and Palamon fig[ht] for Emily, bu[t] Arcite dies i[n] the end

Speaking

21st Century Skills

1 In Chapter 2, Arcite and Palamon both have a dream before their fight. Discuss these questions with a partner.

1 How often do you dream?
2 What do you dream about?
3 What time do you usually go to bed?
4 How many hours do you usually sleep?
5 On Sundays, do you get up early or do you stay in bed until late?
6 Which part of the day do you like best: the morning, the afternoon or the evening? Why?
7 What's your bedroom like?

Reading Comprehension

2 Read the sentences and cross out the incorrect word.

Palamon looked out of the window *and* / ~~*because*~~ he saw Emily.

1 Arcite went home *because* / *but* Palmon stayed in prison.
2 Palamon couldn't leave the prison *because* / *and* he was very sad about this.
3 In Thebes, Arcite was sad *because* / *and* he didn't eat, drink or sleep very much.
4 Arcite waited for two years in Thebes *and* / *because* then he went back to Athens.
5 In Athens, Arcite worked for the King *and* / *but* the King liked Arcite very much.
6 Arcite went to the forest *but* / *because* he didn't know that Palamon was there.

Writing

3 Read this conversation between Arcite and Palamon in the forest. Put the verbs in the correct form.

Arcite: I stayed (stay) in Thebes for two years. Then I came back to Athens. I (**1**) ___ (not eat) very much in Thebes. I (**2**) ___ (be) very sad.
Palamon: Did you (**3**) ___ (come) back for Emily?
Arcite: Yes I did. Now I (**4**) ___ (work) for the King.
He (**5**) ___ (not know) my real name. I often think of Emily. I love her.
Palamon: That's why I'm in the forest.

Before-reading Activities

Reading and Writing MOVERS

The Clerk's Tale
'My story is about a King who has many secrets.'

4 Look at this picture from Chapter 3. Complete the sentences and answer the questions.

The woman is wearing a crown on her head.
1 The man has long brown ___.
2 Whose eyes are closed? ___
3 How many children are there in the picture? ___
4 What's the man doing? ___

Listening

5 **5 Listen to the first part of Chapter 3. Tick (✓) the ones that are true.**

- ☑ This is a story about a King called Walter.
1 ☐ Walter wanted to marry Griselda.
2 ☐ Everybody knew this.
3 ☐ Griselda had a lot of money.
4 ☐ Griselda lived with her father.

Chapter 3

The Clerk's Tale

The Clerk's story is about a King who has a secret. He wants to marry a poor young woman called Griselda.

5 The Clerk was the next person to tell his story. "I have an interesting story," he said. "It's about a King called Walter. He was the King of Saluce, in Italy. Walter wanted to marry a woman, but only he knew the name of this woman. It was a secret. The woman's name was Griselda. She was young and beautiful and she was very nice. She was very poor and she lived in a small house with her father. She cooked and cleaned for him every day. Now here's their story," said the Clerk.

6 One day, Griselda was at home with her father. 'Today is the day,' said Griselda. 'Today we'll know the name of the King's wife. Who can it be? It's very exciting.'

'I think his wife will be a rich woman,' said Griselda's father. But Griselda's father was wrong. Soon he heard somebody at the door. Griselda's father opened the door. He saw Walter, the King of Saluce.

'I want to speak to you. I want to marry Griselda,' said Walter.

'Griselda? M-m-m-my Griselda?' said the father. 'But this is strange. We're poor. And you're the King. Why do you want a poor wife?'

Everyone thinks the King wants to marry a rich woman but he wants Griselda as his wife and she says yes.

'That's not important,' said Walter. 'She's the woman I love. Can I speak to her?'

'Well, of course,' said the father.

Then Walter went inside the house and he spoke to Griselda. 'Griselda,' said Walter. 'Do you want to be my wife? You must do everything I say.'

'I'm too poor for you,' said Griselda. 'I cook and clean. I work hard. I have a different kind of life. But, I want you to be happy. So yes, I want to be your wife. I promise[1] to do everything you say.'

'That's good!' said Walter. So Griselda went home with Walter. Servants arrived. They gave Griselda a beautiful dress and on that day, Walter married Griselda.

Walter and Griselda were very happy. The people of the city liked her. Soon, Griselda had a beautiful baby girl. Walter was also happy. But he

[1] **to promise** to say that you'll do something

Walter and Griselda are happy and have a baby girl, but the King is worried that Griselda only wants to be with him because he's the King.

was worried about something, 'Griselda is very nice,' he thought. 'But, does she love me? Is she only nice because I'm the King? I have to know that she loves me.' Then, Walter did something very bad.

One night, Griselda was in her room. She was with her daughter. Walter's servant came into her room. 'I'm sorry, it's late,' said the servant. 'But I must do what the King says. I must take your daughter.'

The King sends his daughter to Milan to live with his sister, but nobody has to know this. But Griselda doesn't change. She doesn't hate her husband for taking her daughter away.

The servant took the child from Griselda. Griselda was very worried. 'What does he want to do with my daughter? Does he want to kill her?' thought Griselda. But Griselda said nothing. 'Now go!' said Griselda to the servant. 'Do what the King says.'

Then the servant took the child to Walter. 'Don't tell anybody about this,' said Walter to his servant. 'Go with my daughter to Milan. She can live with my sister. But remember! It's a secret. Nobody must know that this girl is my daughter.' Then the King's servant took the child to Milan.

What did Griselda do? Did she hate[1] her husband? The answer to this question is no. Griselda didn't change.

[1] **to hate** to not like

'Does Griselda love me or not,' thought the King. 'Oh, I don't know!'

• • •

After five years, Griselda had another baby. It was a boy. Griselda was happy again, but Walter wasn't happy. 'Griselda,' said Walter. 'Do you promise that you'll always love me?'

5 years pass and Griselda has another baby, a boy but the King still doesn't know if she really loves him. He takes her son away from her too.

'Yes, I do,' said Griselda. 'I'm your wife. I left my old life. I left my house, and my father. Do you want me to die for you? Is that what you want?'

But Walter wasn't happy. 'I have to know that she loves me,' he thought.

Soon, Griselda's son was two years old. One night, Griselda was in her room. She was with her son. Then, the servant came into her room again.

'I must take your son,' he said. 'It's what the King wants.'

'First my daughter, and now my son,' thought Griselda. 'Oh, my children! What does Walter want to do to my son?' Griselda said goodbye to her son. The servant took the child to Walter.

'Take my son to Bologna,' said Walter. 'And

The King sends the boy to Bologna. Griselda doesn't change. She still loves the King even if she doesn't understand why he took her children away from her.

remember, this must be a secret.' Then the servant left. He took the boy to a family in Bologna. 'Now let's see,' thought the King. 'Can Griselda love me now?'

But Griselda didn't change. She didn't hate Walter. She was good to him. 'I don't know what Walter is thinking,' thought Griselda. I promised to love him and I will love him. But why does he do these bad things?'

• • •

Their daughter is now 18 but the King still doesn't know if Griselda loves him. He tells Griselda he wants a new wife, She says nothing.

For some years, Walter was happy. His daughter was in Milan. She was now 18 years old. Walter began to worry again. 'Does Griselda love me?' he thought again. Then he did another bad thing. The King called for Griselda, and he said to her, 'I don't need you any more. I want a new wife.' Griselda said nothing. Then she left Walter's room.

Walter then spoke to his servant. 'Bring me my son and daughter,' he said. 'But it must be a secret. Don't tell anybody who these children are. Everybody must think that I want to marry

›

Griselda is sad because the King tell his servant to take her children awa from her

The King tells a servant to bring back his son and daughter, but nobody knows who they are. Everybody must think that he wants to marry the girl, his daughter, even if it isn't true.

The King sends Griselda away. She must leave her nice clothes for his new wife. Griselda thanks the King for everything and goes back to her father. Then the King asks her to clean the room for his new wife and Griselda does it.

the girl. Of course, I don't want to marry her. She's my daughter, but nobody must know this.'

That afternoon, Walter spoke to Griselda again. 'Griselda, a poor woman can't be my wife. I was wrong,' he said. 'My new wife is arriving. You must go back to your father's home. Leave your clothes here! I can give them to my new wife.'

'Thank you for everything,' said Griselda. 'I'll go home to my father. He's old. I want you to be happy with your new wife.' Then she left the room.

The King was very sad. 'I hate doing this,' he thought. 'I love her so much but I must know that she loves me.'

The next day, Walter went to Griselda's house. He wanted to ask Griselda something. 'Griselda, as you know, my new wife is arriving,' said Walter. 'I need somebody to clean her room. Can you help me?'

'I'm be happy to help,' said Griselda. And then she went to Walter's house. She cleaned the rooms. She made the beds. And she washed the plates.

That morning, Griselda's son and daughter arrived. When Griselda saw the girl she thought, 'She's beautiful,' and she thought of her daughter. 'My daughter is the same age,' she thought. And when Griselda saw the boy, she thought of her son, 'The boy is so clever. My son is the same age.' Of course, she didn't know, that they were her children.'

When Griselda saw the King she said, 'That girl is very nice. She's beautiful. Be nice to her. I hope you can be happy.'

'Stop this!' said the King. 'I don't want to do this any more! My dear wife Griselda. I love you very much! Griselda. You're my wife, and you're perfect.' And then Walter called for his son and daughter.

'Griselda, this is our daughter, and not my new wife. This is our son. I'm very sorry. I only wanted you to love me. Now I know that you do. These are our children!'

Griselda was happy to see her children again. 'Thank you, thank you!' said Griselda. 'My children are safe.'

That night they had a big party. Griselda and Walter were both very happy. And Walter never worried about Griselda's love again.

In the end, the King tells Griselda that the boy and girl are their children and they all have a happy life together.

Think

What do you think of Griselda?

Reading Comprehension

1 Read the sentences. Cross out the incorrect word(s).

Griselda ~~*knows*~~ / *doesn't know* that Walter wants her as his wife.

1 Walter *knows* / *doesn't know* that Griselda loves him.

2 Griselda *knows* / *doesn't know* that her daughter is in Milan.

3 Walter's servant *knows* / *doesn't know* that Griselda's son is in Bologna.

4 Griselda's daughter *knows* / *doesn't know* that Griselda is her mother.

Grammar

2 Read what Walter says and cross out the incorrect word.

Don't *tell* / ~~*say*~~ anybody about this!

1 *Go* / *Bring* to Milan with my daughter!

2 '*Leave* / *Take* my son to Bologna!'

3 '*Bring* / *Take* me my son and daughter!'

4 '*Leave* / *Have* your clothes here!'

5 '*Tell* / *Stop* this!'

3 Re-write the sentences below.

The tale of the clerk *The clerk's tale*

1 The name of the woman. ______________________

2 The wife of the King. ______________________

3 The house of Griselda. ______________________

4 The servant of Walter. ______________________

5 The son of Griselda. ______________________

Writing

21st Century Skills

4 In Chapter 3, the King does a lot of bad things but Griselda's love for him never changes and she never gets angry with him. Discuss these questions with a partner, then write your answers.

1 What makes you angry?
2 When does your family get angry with you?
3 When do you get angry with your friends?
4 Do you feel happier when you're with your family or with your friends? Why?
5 What makes you feel sad?
6 Who do you talk to when you're sad?

Before-reading Activities

Reading and Writing MOVERS

The Merchant's Tale

'My story is sad. It's about an old man who can't see.'

5 Look at this picture from Chapter 4. Complete the sentences and answer the questions.

The servant is carrying a lot of ___food___ .
1 The girl is wearing a green and yellow ________ .
2 Is the man with long brown hair taller than the girl? ________
3 How many people are there in the picture? ________
4 What's the man doing? ________

Listening

7 **6 Listen to the first part of Chapter 4. One statement is false. Which one is it? Tick true or false.**

	T	F
The Merchant has a wife.	✓	☐
1 The Merchant's story is about a young man.	☐	☐
2 The man's name is January.	☐	☐
3 January wants to marry a young woman.	☐	☐
4 January's wife is beautiful.	☐	☐

Chapter 4

The Merchant's Tale

7 The Merchant told the next story. "I travel a lot," he said. "Everywhere I go, I see that people are sad. I have a wife, but do you think I'm happy? Well, I'm not happy. My wife isn't a nice person. I hate my life. I want to tell you a story about a husband and wife. It's a story about a rich, old man. His name's January. January wanted to find a wife. He asked his friends to help him."

The Merchant isn't happy. His story is about an old man called January who wants to find a wife. His friends find him a poor, young girl to marry.

'Don't find me an old wife,' said January. 'I want a young wife.'

January's friends found a wife for him. Her name was May. She was young, but she didn't have any money.

January was very happy with his wife. 'I'm old,' he thought, but now I've got a young wife. I don't have any more problems. May is very beautiful.'

8 But there was another person who thought that

May was beautiful. It was January's servant. His name was Damien. Damien thought of May all the time. He didn't sleep very much. He didn't want to eat. He loved May and now, he had to see her every day, with January! Soon Damien wasn't well. He didn't want to go to work any more. He stayed in bed. In bed, he wrote a letter to May. Then he put the letter in a small bag.

January's servant, Damien loves May. He can't eat or sleep any more because he sees her with January every day. One evening, Damien gives May a love letter.

That evening, January went to dinner. 'Where's my servant, Damien?' he asked.

'Damien isn't well,' said another servant. 'He's in bed now.'

'I'm sorry about that,' said January. 'He's a good servant. He works hard. I want to speak to him.' After dinner, May and January visited Damien. May went to see Damien first. She sat next to him.

'How are you?' asked May.

Damien didn't say anything. He took the letter out of his bag and gave the letter to May. 'Don't speak to anybody about this letter,' he said.

When May was at home, she read Damien's letter. It was a love letter. May didn't know what to do. 'Damien doesn't know my secret,' she thought. 'I love Damien, but he's poor and my husband is rich. How can I help Damien? I want him to be well again,' thought May.

May loves Damien but he's poor and her husband is rich. She gives Damien a letter. Damien feels better after reading the letter.

May wrote a letter to Damien, then she visited him again. She gave Damien the letter. 'Get well soon Damien,' she said. And then she left.

Damien read the letter. The letter changed him. Soon he was well again. The next morning, Damien got up. Now he was happy. Now he wanted to go to work.

January had a big house and he had a beautiful garden. He often went there. It was his favourite place. Only January and May could go to the garden. January had a key. He used the key to go into the garden.

One day January is in the garden and he doesn't feel well. He can't see any more.

One day, January was in his garden. He looked at the trees and the flowers. It was a beautiful day. The weather was perfect. But January didn't feel very well. 'Help! Help!' said January. 'I can't see. I can't see anything! I'm blind[1]!' It was very sad. January couldn't see any more. May went to the

January and his young wife, May ar[e] in the garde[n] January's favourite place.

[1] **blind** you're blind when you can't see

After going blind, January wants May to stay with him all the time. Damien and May write love letters to each other, but they can't speak to each other because January is always there.

garden and she took January back to the house. January stayed in his room for two months. He didn't want to go out and he often thought about May. 'What about May?' he thought. 'Now I can't see my beautiful wife. What's she doing? I can't see what she's doing. Does she love me? I know what to do. I want to tell her that she must always stay in the house. We can stay here together.'

The next day, January said to May, 'You must always sit next to me so I know what you're doing. Sometimes we can go to the garden but we must go there together.'

Now it was May who was sad. Her house was her prison. She thought more and more about Damien.

Damien was also sad. 'I can't speak to May,' he thought. 'January is always there. I must do something. I need to speak to May.' May and Damien often wrote letters to each other. They wrote about their love. But Damien wanted more; he wanted to speak to May. He wrote a letter to her. In the letter he wrote:

May, take a key to the garden. Then give the key to me. January has a lot of keys. Then tell January that you want to go the garden. Do it now!

Damien gave the letter to May, and May did what Damien asked. She gave him the key.

Then Damien went to the garden. He waited there for January and May.

Soon January and May were in the garden. January was happy again. 'I'm old, and I can't see,' he said to May. 'But I have you, my love. I love you so much. And I want to show you how much I love you. Tomorrow, I want to give you all my money and this house and the garden.

'January, what are you saying?' said May. You're the only man in my life.' But of course, there was another man in May's life and that man was Damien. And now she saw Damien in the garden.

'I'm hungry!' said May. 'I want to go to the apple tree. Then I can eat an apple. Wait here!' But May didn't want any apples. She didn't go to the tree. She ran to meet Damien.

January waited for May. He didn't know where

May gives the key to the garden to Damien. Then she goes to the garden with January. January says he wants to give May his house, his garden and all his money. May says she wants an apple but really she wants to run to Damien in the garden.

January can see again and he sees May with a man. But Damien runs away and May says that there's no other man in the garden.

she was. Now, she was with Damien. But then everything changed.

'I can see again, I can see!' said January to himself. 'How is this possible?' he thought. January didn't understand. 'I must tell May; she'll be so happy.' January looked at the apple tree, but May wasn't there. 'Where's May?' thought January. And then he saw her, but he didn't only see May. He also saw a man. 'Who are you? What are you doing? Leave this garden now!' said January. Damien and May looked at January.

'I think he can see us,' said Damien. Then Damien ran. He was very fast and soon he was outside the garden. Then May ran to speak to January.

'What is it my love?' she asked.

'I can see now. I was so happy. I wanted to tell you. And then I saw you with a man. I think I saw you with somebody.'

'You can see again!' said May. 'I'm so happy. But, what are you talking about? A man! You can look everywhere in this garden, but you can't see a man, because there is no man.'

'I was excited that I could see again,' said January. 'I think I saw something that wasn't there, but I thought there was somebody with you.'

'There was no man,' said May. 'Nobody can come into the garden. I want to go back home, my love. Then you can sleep. You're tired.'

'Yes, you're right,' said January. 'Of course, there wasn't a man. Nobody can come into the garden. I want to go home now. We have to tell everybody. We must have a party. Isn't it great? I'm not blind. I can see again!'

"And here my story ends," said the Merchant. "January was happy. He could see again. But there was something that January couldn't see: he couldn't see that May didn't love him and that May loved Damien. January wasn't blind any more. But love is always blind."

January is happy again because he thinks that only he has the key to the garden so he was wrong to think May was with someone else. He can see again but love is blind and he can't see that May doesn't love him.

Think

Do you feel sorry for January? Why? / Why not?

Speaking

1 In Chapter 4, the Merchant says 'love is always blind'. Answer these questions with a partner.

21st Century Skills

1 What do you think 'love is always blind' means?
2 Do you think it's true? Why? / Why not?
3 May and Damien write letters to each other. Do you ever write letters? Why? / Why not?
4 May is much younger than January. Are all your friends the same age as you?
5 What do you look for in a friend?
6 What do you do with your friends in your free time?

Reading Comprehension

2 Number these sentences from Chapter 4 in the right order.

a ☐ Damien writes May a letter.
b ☐ January is blind.
c [1] January finds a wife.
d ☐ May and January go to the garden.
e ☐ Damien runs out of the garden.
f ☐ January can see again.
g ☐ May writes Damien a letter.
h ☐ Damien goes to the garden.

Writing

3 Write the sentences in exercise 2, using the past form of the verb.

January found a wife ______.
______.
______.
______.
______.
______.

Grammar

4 Complete May's letter to Damien using the verbs in the box.

~~be~~	go	love	see	stop

Dear Damien,

*I'm very worried about you. You know I (**1**) ________ you, but, we're both poor. That's why January is my husband and not you. You must (**2**) ________ being so sad. I need to (**3**) ________ you again. You're very important to me. (**4**) ________ back to work for January.*

May

Before-reading Activities

Reading and Writing MOVERS

The Franklin's Tale

'My story is very interesting. It's about a woman who doesn't like the sea.'

5 Look at this picture from Chapter 5. Complete the sentences and answer the questions.

The sun has a face.

1 There's a boat in the ________.

2 Is the woman happy or sad? ________

3 How many sails does the ship have? ________

4 What's the woman doing? ________

Listening

9 **6 Listen to the first part of Chapter 5, and complete the sentences.**

"My story is also about a husband and wife, but, this story is different from the Merchant's story. In my story, love isn't blind. The husband and wife in my story are in (**1**) ______. The wife's name was Dorigen. She loved her (**2**) ______ very much. The husband's name was Arviragus. He was a knight. They lived in France, but, when I start my story, Arviragus was in England. Dorigen was very (**3**) ______. She thought about her husband every day and she (**4**) ______ at home."

Chapter 5

The Franklin's Tale

9 Everybody in the group was tired. It was the end of a long day. They were ready to listen to the Franklin's story.

The Franklin's story is about a husband and wife who love each other. The husband is in England and his wife is waiting for him to come back to France.

"My story is also about a husband and wife. This story is different from the Merchant's story. In my story, love isn't blind. The husband and wife in my story are in love. The wife's name was Dorigen. She loved her husband very much. The husband's name was Arviragus. He was a knight. They lived in France. When I start my story, Arviragus was in England. Dorigen was very sad. She thought about her husband every day. She stayed at home."

10 Arviragus wrote a letter to Dorigen,

'*Don't worry! I'm coming home soon,*' he wrote.

Dorigen read the letter. 'I don't want him to come back soon. I want him to come back now,' she thought. 'But I must go out. I must try to be happy.'

And so, Dorigen started going out. Her house was near the sea. She often went for a walk there with her friends. She always wanted to look at the sea. 'Where's the boat,' thought Dorigen, 'to bring me my husband.' She sometimes looked at the big black rocks[1] in the sea. 'I don't like the sea,' said Dorigen to her friends. 'Look at those black rocks. They're dangerous[2].'

Dorigen's friends were very worried. 'You must stop thinking about those dangerous black rocks,' they said. And so Dorigen's friends took her to a dance. But, she didn't want to dance. At the dance, there was a man called Aurelius. He loved Dorigen. He wanted to speak to her. 'Dorigen, you don't know me very well. My name is Aurelius. You're so beautiful. Is there a place in your heart[3] for me?'

Dorigen looked at Aurelius and said, 'No, there isn't. I love my husband.'

'But what can I do? I need you!' said Aurelius.

'I'm sorry!' said Dorigen.

'But,' said Aurelius, 'is there anything I can do?'

Dorigen is worried about the rocks in the sea so her friends take her to a dance to stop her thinking about them. She meets a man there called Aurelius who loves her but Dorigen loves her husband.

[1] **black rocks** look at the picture on page 53. The black rocks are in the sea

[2] **dangerous** not safe

[3] **heart** 

'Hmm, well, I want the black rocks in the sea to disappear[1]. Do this, and then I can have a place in my heart for you.'

If Aurelius wants Dorigen to love him then she says he must make the rocks in the sea disappear. Aurelius is sad because this is impossible to do.

'But that's not possible,' said Aurelius. 'Nobody can do this!'

'I know,' said Dorigen.

Aurelius went home. At home he said a prayer. 'Help me!' he said. Then he went to bed. And he stayed at home. He never went out: he didn't want to see anybody.

Soon Dorigen's husband came home. Dorigen and Arviragus were together again. Aurelius was at home; he was always at home.

One day, Aurelius read an interesting book. It was a book about magic[2]. 'I can use magic. With magic, I can make the black rocks disappear,' thought Aurelius. 'I know a man in Orléans. His name is Simon. He's famous for his magic. I can ask him to help me.' The next day, Aurelius went to Simon's house.

Aurelius asks his friend Simon to help him make the rocks disappear with magic.

'Hello,' said Simon. 'Have dinner with me, and you can tell me everything.' At dinner there was every kind of food. There was meat, fish, fruit and

[1] **to disappear** when something is not there any more
[2] **magic** what Harry Potter or Merlin do

vegetables. They ate, and Aurelius told Simon his story.

Simon says he can help Aurelius but Aurelius must pay him a lot of money. Two days later they go to the sea and the rock aren't there any more and Aurelius is happy.

Simon listened to the story. And then he said, 'It's true that I sometimes do magic. Now I want to do some magic for you!' And then, the food on the table disappeared.

Aurelius was very happy. 'Can you help me?' asked Aurelius. 'With the black rocks?'

'Yes, I can,' said Simon. 'But, it's expensive. You have to pay me a thousand pounds[1].'

'That's a lot of money,' said Aurelius. 'But, alright. You must be quick. I want to go home tomorrow.'

In the morning, they went back to Aurelius's house. Simon started work and, after two days, he was ready. 'Aurelius,' he said. 'We can go and see the black rocks.' They went to the sea, but when they arrived the black rocks weren't there any more.

'Oh thank you! Thank you so much!' said Aurelius. 'I must show this to Dorigen.'

The next day, Aurelius met Dorigen. 'Hello

›

Aurelius is thinking abo how some magic can help him ma the rocks disappear.

[1] **pounds** English money

VII

Dorigen,' he said. 'Do you remember our conversation about the dangerous black rocks? Do you remember what you promised? Please tell me that you remember.'

'Yes, I remember,' said Dorigen.

'Well,' said Aurelius. 'The black rocks aren't there any more. Come and see!'

Aurelius takes Dorigen to the sea. There are no rocks anymore. Dorigen doesn't know what to do. Then she tells her husband everything and he says she must leave him and go to Aurelius because she promised to do so.

When they arrived, Dorigen looked at the sea. Then she said, 'But, how can black rocks disappear? What can I do? I have to speak to my husband.' And then she ran back home.

When Dorigen arrived home, she started to think. 'I made a promise and promises are important. But I can never do anything bad to my husband. What can I do?' For two days, Dorigen thought about her problem. 'What can I say to my husband?' she thought. Then Dorigen spoke to her husband. She told him everything.

'Don't worry,' said Arviragus. 'You did nothing wrong. But, you promised this to Aurelius. And that's why you must leave me.'

'But I love you Arviragus!' said Dorigen. 'Oh,

what can I do?' Dorigen went to a garden. She needed to think. When she was in the garden, a man spoke to her,

'Hello, where are you going?' It was Aurelius.

'I don't know,' said Dorigen. 'My husband says I must leave him. The black rocks aren't there any more and I promised to be with you.' Dorigen was very sad.

Dorigen stopped speaking and something changed inside Aurelius' heart. 'I hate to see you this sad,' he said. 'Your husband is a good man. You and Arviragus have a perfect love. I must stop this. Go home to your husband. We can forget about your promise.'

'Thank you Aurelius! Thank you! Oh, I'm so happy!' said Dorigen. She went home to tell her husband.

Then, Aurelius remembered something. 'I have to pay Simon a thousand pounds. I only have five hundred pounds. What can I do? I can take him five hundred pounds. I think he'll understand.'

Aurelius went back to Simon's house. Aurelius was very worried.

Aurelius meets Dorigen and when he sees how sad she is, he tells her to forget the promise and go back to her husband. But now Aurelius must pay Simon and he only has five hundred pounds not one thousand.

'Hello!' said Simon. 'Do you have my money?'

'I can give you five hundred pounds,' said Aurelius.

When Simon hears Aurelius' story he says that they're all good people so he doesn't want the money for his magic.

'Why don't you pay me everything? I did everything you asked of me, didn't I? The black rocks disappeared.'

'Yes, they did,' said Aurelius. 'I'm very sorry about the money.' Then Aurelius told Simon everything. He told him about Dorigen and Arviragus. He told him about their perfect love.

'You're all very good people,' said the man. 'You did a very good thing. You have a good heart. I want to be good as well. You forgot about Dorigen's promise, so I want to forget about the thousand pounds. I don't want to take any money from you.'

'Thank you, Simon,' said Aurelius. Aurelius went home. 'I can never be with Dorigen,' he thought. 'But I'm happy because I did a good thing.'

"And that is the end of my story," said the Franklin. "As you can see, it's different from the Merchant's story. This story tells us that there are also many good people in the world."

Think

Which person in this story did you like best? Why?

Reading Comprehension

1 Read the sentences and cross out the incorrect word.

Dorigen *always* / ~~*sometimes*~~ thought about her husband.

1 Dorigen *often* / *never* went for a walk with her friends.

2 Dorigen *always* / *never* wanted to look at the sea.

3 Dorigen *sometimes* / *never* looked at the black rocks.

4 Aurelius *often* / *never* went out.

5 Simon *never* / *often* did magic.

Writing

2 Complete the questions and then complete the answers.

how much what where who why

Where did Dorigen's husband go?
He went to England.

1 ______ didn't like the black rocks in the sea?
______ didn't like them.

2 ______ did Dorigen and her friends go?
______ to a dance.

3 ______ did Dorigen meet at the dance?
______ Aurelius.

4 ______ did Aurelius say to Dorigen?
______ that he loved her.

5 ______ did Simon want for his magic?
______ a thousand pounds.

6 ______ did Aurelius forget Dorigen's promise?
Because Dorigen loved ______ .

Speaking

3 Answer these questions about the Franklin's story with a partner.

21st Century Skills

1 Why do you think Dorigen was worried about the big black rocks in the sea?

2 How often do you go to the beach? What do you like doing there?

3 Dorigen's friends take her to a dance to stop her thinking about the rocks. What do you do to help your friends when they're worried?

4 Simon uses his magic to help Aurelius. What other stories do you know where people use magic?

5 Why does Aurelius tell Dorigen to forget about her promise?

6 Dorigen says promises are important. Do you think the same? Why? / Why not?

Before-reading Activities

Reading and Writing **MOVERS**

The Pardoner's Tale

'My story is about three people who do something very bad.'

4 Look at this picture from Chapter 6. Complete the sentences and answer the questions.

There are three *houses*.

1 The dead man has red __________.

2 The man on the right is wearing a red __________.

3 What are the two men doing? __________

Listening

11 **5 What do these people do in the last chapter of this book?**

The story is about *two* / ~~*three*~~ men.

1 *Ames* / *Lucien* talked a lot.

2 The men wanted to *find a wife* / *get money*.

3 The men *were* / *weren't* friends.

4 The men were in *an inn* / *a garden*.

Chapter 6

The Pardoner's Tale

11 "Now I have a story for you," said the Pardoner to the other people in the group. "It's a story about three men. They were called Ames, Lucien and Morise. Ames talked a lot. The other two men didn't talk very much. These men were very bad. They only thought about money. They were always together, but they weren't friends. Friends help you. Friends listen to your problems. They were greedy[1], and they had no love in their hearts. My story begins in an inn. The three men were together at a table near the window."

The Pardoner's story is about three bad men who aren't really friends and only think about money.

12 'I'm hungry!' said Ames.

'So am I,' said Lucien. 'I want something to eat.' But then Ames saw something strange.

'Look!' he said. 'Look out of the window! What are those two men doing?'

'Oh, yes!' said Lucien. 'They're carrying a man.'

'Yes, you're right,' said Ames. 'Who is he? I

The three men look out of the window and see two men carrying a man.

Ames, Lucier and Morise are looking out of the window and they see two men carrying dead man.

[1] **greedy** to always want more and more

think we know him. Yes, it's Adranus the innkeeper!' said Ames. 'Is that Adranus?'

'Yes, it is. Adranus died last night. Somebody killed him,' said the innkeeper.

The innkeeper says Death killed Adranus and the three men want to find him. The innkeeper says Death is very dangerous but the men don't listen.

'Who did this to Adranus?' asked Ames.

'Death[1] did it!' said the innkeeper.

'Death! That's a strange name,' said Ames. 'Why is he called Death?'

'Because of the things he does,' said the innkeeper. 'Last week he met five people. He killed them all. Nobody can find him. Everybody is worried about Death.'

'Let's look for him!' said Ames. 'It could be fun. We must find him, and we must fight this strange man called Death.'

'Don't do it!' said the innkeeper. 'He's very dangerous.'

'Don't worry! We know what to do,' said Ames.

'People say that Death lives near the mountain[2],' said the innkeeper. 'Don't go near the mountain if you don't want to be the next people to die.'

1 **death** when you die. Death is the noun for the verb to die
2 **mountain** 

'Well we're going to the mountain. Nothing can stop us.' So the three men left the inn. They started walking to the mountain.

The three men walked for a long time. They often had to stop. After some time, the three men met an old man.

An old man tells them that Death puts money in a bag near an old tree. He tells them not to go there but they don't listen to him. They want the money.

'Hey, old man!' said Ames.

'What do you want?' said the old man.

'Do you know a man called Death?'

'Yes, I know about him,' said the old man. 'But why are you asking me this? Don't go near that man! He's dangerous.'

'Tell us where we can find him,' said Ames

'Nobody knows where he is,' said the old man. 'But people say he often goes somewhere. They say that he puts his money there.'

'Money!' said Ames. 'Where is this place?'

'Before you walk up the mountain there's a very old tree. It's near the road which goes to the mountain. Sometimes he goes there. They say he's got a lot of money.'

'I think I know where this tree is,' said Ames. 'We can go there now!'

'No! Stop!' said the old man. But it was too late. The friends wanted to find the tree.

The three men find the bag where Death puts his money. Ames and Lucien wait with the bag and Morise goes to the town for some food.

After two hours, they arrived at the place. And they saw the tree. 'I want to look for the money now,' said Ames. 'Do you remember? The old man said that Death put it here.' They looked for the money, and soon they found it. It was under a small rock. There was a lot of money in a big bag. The bag was very difficult to carry.

'Here it is! Look how much there is! We're rich,' said Ames.

'Hooray!' they said. 'We've got a lot of money!' They were very excited.

'I want to get something to eat and drink,' said Ames.

'OK,' said Lucien. 'We can go to the town and buy something.'

'But, wait,' said Ames. 'Two of us must wait here with the money. Morise, you go to the town. We can wait for you here.'

'OK,' said Morise. And he went to the town. The other two men waited under the tree. After an hour, Ames thought of something. 'Listen!' said Ames. 'There's a lot of money in that bag.'

'Yes, you're right,' said Lucien. 'There's about six hundred pounds. That's two hundred pounds each.'

Ames and Lucien want to kill Morise so they can have more money.

'Yes, but I think we can have three hundred pounds each.'

'How?' asked Lucien.

'Well, we can kill Morise when he comes back. Then we can have more money.'

'Yes! I want to do that!' said Lucien. So the two men waited for Morise.

Morise was near the town. He started thinking. 'Well, there's about six hundred pounds in that bag. That's about two hundred pounds for me. Two hundred pounds is a lot of money. But six hundred pounds is much more. Six hundred pounds can change my life. I know what to do. I must kill Ames and Lucien. Then I can have all the money.'

Ten minutes later, Morise arrived at the town. He bought some food and drink. But he also bought some poison[1]. He put the

[1] **poison** don't drink this because you will die

Morise is greedy and wants all the money for himself so he buys some poison to kill Ames and Lucien.

Ames and Lucien kill Morise but then they die too because they drink the poison that Morise put in the drink.

poison in the drink, then he went back to the tree. It was getting late when Morise arrived. 'Ames, Lucien, I've got the food and ...' And they were the last words that Morise spoke, because then Ames and Lucien killed him.

'Now we have more money,' said Ames. They didn't worry about Morise.

The two men were happy. They drank together. Soon the poison was in their bodies. After a minute, the poison killed them.

"That's the end of my story," said the Pardoner. "The three men wanted to fight Death. They were greedy and that's why they died. I want you to remember this story when we arrive at Canterbury and when we say our prayers."

The others thought it was a very good story. Then the people in the group thought about all the stories. There were a lot of things to think about. After four days, Canterbury was very, very near. ■

Think

What do you think of the Pardoner's story?

Ames and Lucien are dying becau[se] they drank t[he] poison that Morise put i[n] their drink.

After-reading Activities • Chapter 6

Reading Comprehension

1 Choose the correct option.

At the inn the three men want

A ☑ something to eat. B ☐ something to drink.

1 The three men want to look for Death because...

A ☐ they have nothing to do. B ☐ they want to find some money.

2 Where does Death live?

A ☐ near a forest B ☐ near a mountain

3 Who do the men meet when they go to the mountain?

A ☐ an old man B ☐ a friend

4 Where do the men find the money?

A ☐ in a bag B ☐ in a box

5 How much money do they find?

A ☐ two hundred pounds B ☐ six hundred pounds

6 Where does Morise put the poison?

A ☐ in the food B ☐ in the drink

Reading and Writing MOVERS

2 Choose the correct word for each sentence about Chapter 6.

The three men were ___in___ a bar.

~~in~~ on up

1 The men wanted to look ________ a man called Death.

at like for

2 The men walked ________ the mountain.

at to for

3 ________ they arrived at the mountain, they found the money.

How When Why

4 Morise ________ some food and drink.

bought paid went

5 Arnes and Lucien waited ________ Morise to come back.

to at for

Vocabulary

3 Read what the Pardoner says about the three men. Complete the text with the correct adjective.

dangerous happy old greedy ~~excited~~ tired

"Ames, Lucien and Morise were three young men, but, they were very bad. They were *excited* about going to the mountain. They wanted to fight the man called Death, but the innkeeper said that it was (**1**) ________ . On their way to the mountain, they met an (**2**) ________ man. He told them about the money. They arrived at the mountain after many hours. They were (**3**) ________ . But they wanted to look for the money. When they found the money, they were very (**4**) ________ . But then, they became (**5**) ________ . They wanted more."

Writing

4 Think of all the stories in this book. The innkeeper must choose the best story. Which story do you think is the best?

	It was interesting	It was easy to understand
The Prologue	☐	☐
The Knight's Tale	☐	☐
The Clerk's Tale	☐	☐
The Merchant's Tale	☐	☐
The Franklin's Tale	☐	☐
The Pardoner's Tale	☐	☐

21st Century Skills

The best story was ________________

I liked this story because ________________

____

Focus on...

Geoffrey Chaucer

Geoffrey Chaucer

Important for the English language because he wrote in English and not French or Latin like English authors before him did. There are more than 2,000 new English words in *The Canterbury Tales*, like 'village' and 'desk' that people didn't know at that time.

Early life

We don't know much about Chaucer's early life only, that he lived between 1340 and 1400.

1340

1366

Marriage and first jobs

He married Philippa Roet in 1366 and they had three or four children. Philippa Roet worked for the King's wife, the Queen. This helped Chaucer to get important jobs and he worked for King Edward III and King Richard II.

Read these sentences. Write true (T) or false (F) or don't know (dk)

Every person in the book told two stories. [F]
1 Chaucer worked for the Queen of England. [ ]
2 Chaucer was happy when he was a child. [ ]
3 Chaucer began writing *The Canterbury Tales* in 1387. [ ]
4 Chaucer had three or four children. [ ]
5 Chaucer didn't write any other books. [ ]
6 Chaucer met the Italian writer, Boccaccio, in Italy. [ ]

Travel and interests
He travelled to France and Italy for his work. Italy was very important for Chaucer, because he could read the works of the writers Dante and Boccaccio.

1387

First works
His first book was *The Book of the Duchess*. Then he wrote *Parliament of Fowls*, *The Legend of Good Women*, and *Troilus and Criseyde*.
The Canterbury Tales – Chaucer started writing his most famous book in 1387 near Canterbury. He didn't finish *The Canterbury Tales*. At first, he wanted each person in the book to tell two stories, one going to Canterbury and one coming back. But they only tell one story each in the book. Chaucer also never tells us which story the innkeeper chose.

1400

Died
Nobody knows when he died but most people think it was in 1400.

Did you know?

1. Chaucer didn't finish *The Canterbury Tales*. There are some other stories he didn't finish.
2. Chaucer wanted each person in *The Canterbury Tales* to tell two stories: one story when going to Canterbury and another story when coming back to London, but they only tell one story each.
3. On page 71, you chose the best story, but we don't know which story the innkeeper chose. Chaucer didn't tell us.
4. When Chaucer wrote *The Canterbury Tales* he lived near Canterbury, but he wanted to go back to live in London.

Focus on...

Pilgrims on the road to Canterbury

Canterbury in the 1300s

"There were a lot of things to think about.
After four days, Canterbury was very, very near."

Now we can think about our group. They're tired, but they're happy. Now they're arriving in Canterbury. While travelling to Canterbury, they saw villages and towns. These places were small, but Canterbury is different. It's very big. The first thing they see is the city wall. Canterbury is an important place. A lot of people come here.
Now they are inside the city. There's a lot of noise. Canterbury is a very good place to buy things. There are a lot of people who want to buy things that they need. They come from villages and towns near Canterbury. You can buy things in the shops, or on the street. People are buying food. They're buying animals. They're buying clothes. Some people are speaking to our group. They want them to buy something, but the people in our group don't want to buy anything.
They want to go to the Cathedral. The group walks down the street. There are a lot of inns. After visiting the Cathedral, they want to stay in one of these inns. Then they must go back to London, but first they have to see the Cathedral.

Now the group is walking to the cathedral. There are a lot of other people. They're also on a pilgrimage. People are saying their prayers, and they're singing. There it is! The shops and the houses are small, but the cathedral is so big! It's the only thing that you can see, but they have to wait before they can go inside. There are too many people.

A bishop blessing the annual fair or market

The cathedral was an important place. Many people came here on a pilgrimage. In the year 1420, for example, 100,000 people visited the cathedral. People went there to do different things. Today, many people go on holiday every year. Then people went on a pilgrimage every year. It was a kind of holiday for a lot of people. They went to say their prayers. People went on a pilgrimage because they needed something. Some people were not very well. Other people were sorry about something. They wanted to ask God for help.

Canterbury Cathedral

Read this again. Make a list of the things that you can see and hear in Canterbury.

Focus on...

A medieval baker with his apprentice

Food

The Innkeeper: 'Now, Cook, you're famous for your meat pies, with no meat in them. We know that people buy your pies many days after you make them. Tell us your story.' *(From the Cook's Tale)*

One of the other people who went to Canterbury was a cook. A cook is somebody who makes food for other people. That was his job. Chaucer didn't finish the cook's story. The innkeeper didn't think he was a very good cook. Cooks made food for shops or they cooked for rich people. Rich people ate a lot of meat, fish, and white bread. Life was more difficult for people who didn't have much money. They didn't eat a lot of fish or meat. White bread was too expensive. The cook in *The Canterbury Tales* had a shop, but most people couldn't buy things from a shop very often. They had to make their food at home. So what did people eat?

Breakfast Most people ate black bread (see picture). White bread was only for the rich. Black bread wasn't very good. It was very hard and it wasn't very nice to eat. People ate this very early. They ate it at 6 o' clock in the morning because then they had to work.

Lunch More black bread with cheese. Sometimes there was some meat, but meat was very expensive. Most of the time, people ate lunch outside. They worked outside. They didn't have time to go home to eat. The working day was very long and hard.

The cook

Supper People ate supper before they went to bed. When the sun went down, people often ate soup. The soup had a lot of vegetables. It didn't often have meat in it.

Read the sentences. Cross out the incorrect word(s).

Poor people ~~*didn't often eat*~~ / *often ate* meat.

1 Poor people *always* / *never* ate white bread.
2 Rich people *always* / *never* ate dark bread.
3 Poor people *often bought* / *didn't often buy* food.
4 Rich people *sometimes* / *never* ate meat.
5 Rich people *often ate* / *didn't often eat* fish.

Medieval cuisine

Test Yourself

1 Choose the correct answer A, B or C for each question.

Chapter 1: When does Geoffrey arrive at the inn?
A ☐ In the morning **B** ☑ In the afternoon **C** ☐ In the evening

1 *Chapter 2:* Where did the King find Arcite and Palamon?
A ☐ In the mountains **B** ☐ In the forest **C** ☐ In a garden

2 *Chapter 3:* Where does Griselda's daughter go?
A ☐ To Milan **B** ☐ To Rome **C** ☐ To Bologna

3 *Chapter 4:* What doesn't May give Damien?
A ☐ A key **B** ☐ A letter **C** ☐ An apple

4 *Chapter 5:* How much money does Aurelius have?
A ☐ A thousand pounds **B** ☐ Six hundred pounds **C** ☐ Five hundred pounds

5 *Chapter 6:* Who tells Ames, Lucien and Morise about the money?
A ☐ Adranus **B** ☐ The innkeeper **C** ☐ The old man

2 Write the name of the Chapter or Chapters next to each question. In which chapter(s):

do people go to an inn? *The Prologue*
The Pardoner's Tale

1 do people look out of a window? ________ ________
2 does somebody go blind? ________
3 does somebody do magic? ________
4 do people find some money? ________
5 do people write a letter? ________ ________
6 do people fight? ________
7 do people go to a garden? ________ ________
8 do people go to a forest? ________
9 do people go to a mountain? ________
10 do people promise something? ________ ________
11 does somebody die? ________ ________
12 is there a servant? ________ ________
13 is there a King? ________ ________

Syllabus

Topics

Love
Feelings
Family
Friendship
Nature
Stories

Grammar and Structures

Simple Present: states and habits
Present Continuous: actions in progress
Past Simple: finished actions
Future forms: will
Can: ability, permission
Could: ability, permission in the past
Must: obligation
Have to: necessity
Adjectives
Prepositions (place, movement, time)
Pronouns
Question Words
Relative Clauses
There is/There are
Verbs + infinitive/ing

Teen ELi Readers

Stage 1
Maureen Simpson, *In Search of a Missing Friend*
Charles Dickens, *Oliver Twist*
Geoffrey Chaucer, *The Canterbury Tales*
Janet Borsbey & Ruth Swan, *The Boat Race Mystery*
Lucy Maud Montgomery, *Anne of Green Gables*
Mark Twain, *A Connecticut Yankee in King Arthur's Court*
Mark Twain, *The Adventures of Huckleberry Finn*
Angela Tomkinson, *Great Friends!*
Edith Nesbit, *The Railway Children*
Eleanor H. Porter, *Pollyanna*
Anna Sewell, *Black Beauty*
Kenneth Grahame, *The Wind in the Willows*

Stage 2
Elizabeth Ferretti, *Dear Diary…*
Angela Tomkinson, *Loving London*
Mark Twain, *The Adventures of Tom Sawyer*
Mary Flagan, *The Egyptian Souvenir*
Maria Luisa Banfi, *A Faraway World*
Frances Hodgson Burnett, *The Secret Garden*
Robert Louis Stevenson, *Treasure Island*
Elizabeth Ferretti, *Adventure at Haydon Point*
William Shakespeare, *The Tempest*
Angela Tomkinson, *Enjoy New York*
Frances Hodgson Burnett, *Little Lord Fauntleroy*
Michael Lacey Freeman, *Egghead*
Michael Lacey Freeman, *Dot to Dot*
Silvana Sardi, *The Boy with the Red Balloon*
Silvana Sardi, *Scotland is Magic!*
Silvana Sardi, *Garpur: My Iceland*
Silvana Sardi, *Follow your Dreams*
Gabriele Rebagliati, *Naoko: My Japan*

Stage 3
Anna Claudia Ramos, *Expedition Brazil*
Charles Dickens, *David Copperfield*
Mary Flagan, *Val's Diary*
Maureen Simpson, *Destination Karminia*
Anonymous, *Robin Hood*
Jack London, *The Call of the Wild*
Louisa May Alcott, *Little Women*
Gordon Gamlin, *Allan: My Vancouver*